The Art of Erasing Emotions

Techniques to discharge any emotional problems in
men, women and children using EFT and Sedona

Sam Reddington

ISBN-13:
978-1548774516

ISBN-10:
1548774510

Introduction

The purpose of this book is to teach you about two of the most effective techniques in clearing out bad emotional and mental energies from your body. Having the ability to discharge said undesirable emotions and thoughts from your system, will let you live a more peaceful existence. To be free of any negativity trapped in your head and in your body whatever those negativities maybe will lead a more satisfying life free of bad emotions, bad energies, fear, et cetera.

Compared to my other book which I also recommend you get so you can have more options in dealing with these mental and emotional junks, it deals directly with and dislodges said emotions or energetic physiology. This is about unburdening yourself from all these junk hampering or blocking you from accomplishing your goals in life. Some of these things may be difficult to explain why they work just that they do. So suspend your disbelief and assume that they work at least in the meantime although it will work regardless of your belief systems. As long as you execute the techniques fully, then they are guaranteed to work

With that said, it is helpful to think of these emotions and thoughts as things or objects that physically exists. You can move them around, or just drop them out your system if they are being unhelpful to you. These things drag you down and hamper your progress.

The Mystery of Tapping

Unsolved emotional issues often has a means of holding us back from holistic happiness, limits personal performance, beliefs and relationships. These unsolved emotions arouse unpleasant memories and these in turn triggers unpleasant emotions. When these issues remain unresolved it creates negative energies which leads to anxiety, fear, anger, etc. EFT is a unique healing procedure that focuses on creating a balance in the energy flow traversing via the body meridians and channels or pathway in which energy flows.

This technique uses various psychological approaches (cognitive and psychological) including acupuncture and its physical benefits to produces a total treatment to emotional issues including other accompanying issues. A session of Emotional Freedom Techniques comprises of paying detailed attention to the particular problem involved using the tapping techniques on the body's meridian points thus sending emotional balancing vibrations throughout the body. This procedure is suitable for everyone, it is relatively easy and has been proven to cure varieties of problems like phobias, addictions of all kinds, grief, stage fright, Enuresis, relationship issues and the likes. Let's familiarize ourselves with the various tapping points.

You and your body's meridian Points

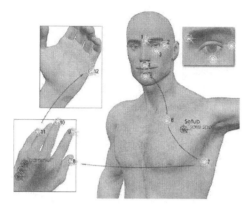

Primarily EFT requires giving heed to any detrimental emotion or any unsolved issues and focusing mentally on the particular issue. The finger tips are used to tap 5-7 times each on the 12 Meridian points situated all over the body (the channels in which energy flows). This is accompanied with a repetition of deliberate positive words or phrases of self acceptance. This will result in resolution as negative energies get expelled from tapping of these points and systemic balance is restored. The 12 meridians are connected to each other which connects the supply of energy flows either upward and downward the body, these meridians are;

Stomach meridian
Heart meridian
Small Intestine meridian
Bladder meridian
Kidney meridian
Pericardium meridian
The Triple Warming meridian
Gallbladder meridian
Liver meridian
Lung meridian
Spleen meridian
Large Intestine meridian

To effectively use EFT, you rub on or maybe tap on the body's meridian points while vocalizing a phrase simultaneously. But before venturing into this, you will have to become familiar with these points.

There are two major points to be tapped and other minor taping points all connected to the body meridian.

The sore spot: The particular spot feels sore when rubbed. This is by virtue of lymphatic congestion (accumulation of blood) which occurs here. To locate it, put your hand right on your chest over your heart. Where your fingertips land, rub gently on the chest (on the Breast bone, below the collar bone) till you find a place that's a little more sensitive than the surrounding areas. There is one on the left side of the chest too. By rubbing on the sore spot you are helping in decongesting the accumulated blood or body fluids.

The karate chop: this can be found on the outer edge (close to the pinky finger) of the hand in the fleshy part just below the pinky finger. Tapping can be done with both hands together simultaneously by crossing your hands on the outer edge of the palms to form a karate chop and bumping the two hands together. The minor points include;

Eye brow: Just above the nose, the tip of the eye brow (on either the left or right one.)
Side of your Eye: Tapping should be done on the bony side of (of either left or right eye) tap on the honey part of the eye socket just at the Corner of the eye. Not too close to the eye and not as far as the temple.
Underneath the Eye: On the bony part of eye socket half an inch from under the pupil.
Beneath the Nose: From the center point of the nose this is between under the nose and the top of the lip.
Chin: Located on the crease in the chin half way between the chin and the lower lip.
Collar Bone: On either side of the collar bone 2 inches before where the breastbone, collarbone, and first rib meet.
Under the Arm: This is located about 4 inches below your armpit either on the left or right part of your body. For females it is the middle of the band of their bras for the males the same line as their nipple.
Top of the Head: Loop back and touch the top of the head.
Wrist: located below the crease of each hands where the hands and wrist join.
Liver: Drawing a line from the nipple just on the lower edge of the ribs.

Now we know where to tap to get our release. These techniques have basically four components. They are:

The set up stage: During tapping on either the sore spot or the karate chop, reflect on that negative emotion or unresolved issue you have a desire to solve. Give the problem a grade level from 0-10. 0 signifies no level while 10 shows the highest level. Then with as much conviction, state your set up phrase while you rub your sore spot or tap on your karate chop. Your set up phrase must be precise and clear. An example could be " even though I am scared of talking to strangers I DEEPLY and COMPLETELY accept and LOVE myself". The essence of this is to link the negative issue while affirming self love and true acceptance! Further explore this as you tap on other meridians. For example, "Yes I suck, for being scared! I hate being scared all the time! I hate it that XYZ and I feel ABC, but that's ok anyway because these problems are getting resolved and I still love and accept myself!" How it works is you're further uncovering layers of that negativity WHILE they are being chopped down, bit by bit and energetically displaced via the tapping actions.

Moving to the Sequence: After concluding the Setup step, place your middle and index finger together. Tap 7 times on each of the meridian points earlier mentioned using your fingertips. Tap gently but firmly, avoid being hard so you don't get bruised. You could switch sides during the tapping sequence alternating between the left and the right. Repeat your starting phrase while taping seven times each on the body meridian points.

The nine Gamut process: It's Location is at the back of either hand is something called gamut point. It is approximately half an inch behind the mid-point in in-between the knuckles at the base of your ring finger and your little finger. This energy is accountable for the feeling despair, anxiety, grief, depression, despair etc.

After concluding the sequence, now you can engage in the 9-Gamut Procedure. Our brain is like a radio to listen to your favorite station, you have to be tuned in to it. This step focuses on tuning in our brain via eye movements to the correct spot necessary for the resolution of the problems. Not only are certain nerves activated in our brains during this eye movement exercise, but this procedure also employs humming any random song. Thereby looking downwards to the left (and humming) and looking at the lower right (while counting 1 to 10) activates both hemispheres of the brain, to effect dislodging of the gunks of emotions. This procedure uses nine brain- stimulating actions performed simultaneously and continuously while tapping the Gamut Points to unlock the balancing of our brain.
steps:
Close your eyes: To calm yourself
Open your eyes: For focus
Turn your Eyes lower right without moving your head (this stimulates memory energizing sensations).
Turn your Eyes down left without moving your head.
Try rolling your eyes clockwise (increases the visual memory and imagination)
Roll the eyes anti-clockwise
Now Hum a song for about 5 seconds (to stimulate and engage the left part of your brain)
Count aloud and clearly 1-5
Hum any song, for about 5 seconds again (this stimulates the right side of your brain)
Go over the sequence: After completing the sequence, concentrate on the problem once more. And take note of how less intense it is now, in comparison to a few minutes earlier. Rate it on the same number scale again. If it is higher than 4 you should start

the round of tapping anew. Continue tapping until either there is a reduction in the intensity or total removal of the problem. The words or phrase at the set up stage can be changed to create a space for your effort to fix the issues and process. Your statement can be in this form "Although I **STILL** have some fears talking to strangers I deeply and completely accept myself".

Emotion: The engine behind it

Emotions are like tiny remote controls in our head operated by someone up there who is in charge of our thinking, behavior and actions. Since emotions control our behaviors it affect not just our physical bodies but also how our body affects our feelings and thinking. Emotions that are not expressed and released but hidden deep within the body can cause illnesses such as ulcer, arthritis, and other chronic diseases.

The Emotion is a succession of electrochemical signals transferred to our brains and interpreted to bring about certain feelings. This emotion is the basis on which decisions are made. For instance a child sees the mom after school, the emotion triggered is joy. The decision upon which the child takes will depend on his feelings. He runs into the mother's arms.

Negative emotions like phobias, cause chemical reactions different from the chemicals released when someone is happy, loved and content. It is no wonder that with depression comes illness. Mr. Jones had a brain tumor and required surgery. As he was getting epileptic fits, his fiancée Hannah stood by him encouraging him and was a constant joy to him. The surgery was successful and Mr. Jones made a remarkable recovery. Two months later he had a relapse. Unfortunately, his fiancée had broken up with him. Some would say he died due to the tumor but it is so clear that he died because he was broken hearted.

Triggers of Emotion

Our emotions are innate and come from deep within us —sometimes seemingly out of nowhere! There are supporting factors which affect these states. These are mainly our sensory experiences; auditory, olfactory, gustatory, tactility, ophthalmic. These also affect and trigger our various thinking processes as well as emotions.

Jane was raped by a homeless man as a teenager while returning from the house of her friend. The man smelled like dirt, and for years Jane experienced difficulty in going close to the trash bin. Her fears where often caused by the smell of garbage which brings her back to that fateful night.

So too the other senses are triggers of emotion. You hear a song, and you get nostalgic recollections of the first meeting you've had with your wife of 15 years. It brings a lovely feeling of nostalgia and love. All these thoughts and feelings do not exist merely in a vacuum. They are products of triggers which rouse emotions, and in turn, an attitude, habit, way of thinking or lifestyle is born.

Darla had this habit of washing her hands if she touched another person. It became crippling and she was unable to stop. She recounts how she found her mother murdered and she felt her blood. This resulted in her paranoia of touching another person.

Working Through the Tangled Web of Emotions

The first step in breaking free from the reactions to negative emotions is identifying them. You just lost your job, you are sad and all of a sudden you can't eat, can't sleep, the thoughts of unpaid bills run through your mind, and this puts you in panic mode. Your emotions along with your similar behaviors would be analyzed thus; Sadness over job loss+ panic over the present+ worry over the future= Stomach ulcer.

A lot of people do not know that identifying their emotions is the initial step to a healthier life. What is the real trigger of the emotion? Do you have the ulcer because you did not eat well enough or because sadness gave an outlet to other negative emotions?

Besides identifying the emotion, we need to learn how to channel them the right way instead of suppressing them. Something bad happens to you, instead of picking a mental shovel and burying it in the sand, only for it to creep out when you least expect it. Why not deal with it once and for all? Avoid exaggerating the problem by making it bigger than it seems. Ignore the committee of negative voices speaking to you. Finally, if letting it go means crying-- big girls do cry, so it's perfectly fine. Tears make endorphins which trigger a positive emotion in the body. No wonder women have attested to feeling better after crying. Working through tangled web of emotions does not mean that one would be happy at all times -- but that when stress and other unpleasant emotions come our way, we will be able to deal with them realistically.

The relationship between the body and emotions.
1. Large intestine meridian: this is affects guilt.
2. The stomach meridian: affected by disgust and greed.

3. Spleen meridian: affected by worry and anxiety over the future.
4. Heart meridian; gets the feeling of pure joy and anger.
5. Small intestine: this feels the effect of insecurity and also sadness
6. Bladder meridian: Affected by fright, restlessness and impatience.
7. Kidney meridian: indecision and fear.
8. Pericardium/circulation: hurt, regret, extreme joy and jealousy.
9. Thyroid meridian: affected by depression, hopelessness and despair.
10. Gall bladder meridian: Feels the effect of rage.
11. Liver meridian: affected by unhappiness and anger.

Emotional Freedom Techniques and Its Effectiveness

To ensure that the issues you tackled in EFT have been resolved, there is a need to conduct a test. To make sure that you did not only experience temporary relief --you should reflect back on the memories, this time with less emotional intensity.

You may notice the following if the tapping session worked:
1. Dropping Shoulders.
2. Feeling Sleepy
3. The feeling of Tiredness
4. A Relief of Pain in a body part that was not targeted during tapping.
5. Grasping (an exhale of surprise)
6. Sighing and yawning (an indication of relief or boredom or energy shift).
7. Tears or watery eyes (can happen from yawning)
8. Coughing or feeling a Lump in the throat.
9. Feeling a Knot in your chest.
10. You could get a buzzing feeling all through the body (this would feel as if an extra source of oxygen is flowing all over the body.)

Another manner of testing the efficiency of the EFT would be through the senses. It was said earlier that the thoughts trigger the emotions. Therefore, if you have a desire to test if your tapping worked, you should put those senses to check. For Jane whose sense of smell triggers her fear and apprehension, after the tapping test, she should go closer to the trash can and see if the intensity has been dramatically reduced.

Furthermore, the effectiveness can be tested through muscle testing which somewhat resembles a lie detector test. The tissue reaction is used in testing how far EFT has been active. A relaxed muscle shows that the issues have been resolved, but a tensed or jerking muscle shows otherwise.

Also, using a live test can show how useful the EFT session was. But, before conducting a real life test make sure the level of intensity is low, for instance, level 3. An individual with stage fright can check the efficiency by doing something that involves public speaking, and the aftermath would show if they have been cured or not.

Disassociated Technique

This method entails recreation of the memory alongside the client participating as an onlooker without reliving the initial experience. That is a client who had suffered a traumatic experience, recreates it and separates the emotions from him. It follows the pattern described below;

Through narration, the client explains his experiences to the therapists. Then the practitioner allows the client to express himself and his fears.
Then with the use of the movie procedure, the client is asked to ascribe a title to the memory that triggers the concerns.
Next, he/she's asked to pick a row in the cinema as he watches himself in the movie. This is called the Cinema method.
Margaret had a traumatic experience when she was a child. She was molested by her relative. But lately, she had been experiencing fear and suppressed rage as she heard of her uncle's death. She describes her experience to her practitioner, and he asks to pick a movie title to which she was unable to give a title. She picked a cinema row in the front and watched the memory reel, while she explained her experience to her practitioner. Then say these words " even though I was hurt and molested, I deeply and completely accept myself." By doing this, she was able to reconcile the emotions and her past. Realize that this is effective because it allows an extra distance or gap for the patient to feel extra safe. Some patients also have a more difficult time picturing traumatic events, unless you make them watch it through an imaginary cinema.

Dealing with hurdles in EFT

Emotional Freedom Technique provides on a larger scale, quicker results than other therapies. New difficulties and unresolved problems might arise during the therapy. These issues may be part of the initial problem or are the undertones. They include:

The reversals: this occurs when there is a total reversal of the energy surge and this keeps a therapy from working. This involves self-defeating and negative thoughts hidden in the subconscious. These ideas have the tendency of defeating the whole purpose of the therapy. In this situation, the individual believes that it is better to remain in their previous situations while investing in self-pity and negative thoughts. To them, their present situation is way better. This clearly shows an individual who is afraid of change. The person could think this way; "what would happen to me if I lose my fear of public speaking?", "would I be liked", "I don't think I have a great personality", "I am not even good at writing speeches." The individual stuck in this form of psychological reversal is unable to move forward because of his fears and losing the secondary gains or benefits from having that problem. For example, on a subconscious level the patient may feel he will lose his newly found friends (perhaps even a potential love interest) in the support group.

The reversal may be caused by physical items hindering the flow of the energy, e.g., a metal piece, a Mobile phone, etc., severe depression or a case of negativity, dehydration, etc. Since water is a major need of the body, if the body is dehydrated, energy flows in the body might flow in the opposite direction. Holding a cell phone close to the body during EFT causes the reversal. EFT uses energy flow, and the cell phone is magnetic and may redirect this energy flow in a wrong way. If the body has incubated too many toxins, it will take a while to evacuate them. But these toxins can cause reversal as the energy surge is not flowing correctly. The person might reverse into a state of pathetic wishful thinking.
Also, EFT might be hindered if the individual is clinging to the problem due to some benefits he/she derives from it. This is called the secondary benefits syndrome.

A series of techniques can be used to stop these reversals. Repeating the karate chops, keeping hydrated, involving oneself in uplifting activities such as listening to music and being positive are examples.

EFT Versus Other Therapies

Emotional Freedom Techniques (EFT) and Thought Field Therapy (TFT).
The both of them are similar in that they both use methods that involve tapping on specific acupressure points while being focused on a particular emotion. The significant difference between the two is that TFT uses a tapping sequence known as an algorithm for each of the different emotional problems. While EFT employs a shorter version for each of the various emotional problems.

TFT was developed in the 1980's by a Dr. Roger Callahan, a cognitive psychologist and hypnotherapist who is also a phobia specialist. While Gary Craig, an ordained minister and Standford engineer, applied Callahan's method to his clients. As the years went by, he simplified the method and found tapping in sequence over all the various meridians unnecessary.

TFT is more complicated due to the multiple tapping required for each meridian for each problem. It's harder to learn and apply, unlike EFT which can be implemented on oneself without another practitioner present.

Emotional Freedom Techniques and Behavioral Kinesiology

Behavioral Kinesiology is the study of muscles and muscular movement (kinesis, motion). It involves combining touch specific body points and the use of manual muscle testing. This has been known to assist in the treatment of mental, physical or even substance abuse problems. Behavioral Kinesiology is a system for assessing the effects of all stimuli both internal and external on the body, thereby enabling us to understand the levels of actions in the body energy system. This aids in assessing the various degrees of stress under which an individual can function. It can lead to the re-balancing of the body and enhancement of body energies as well as correct the emotional imbalances.

The five primary tenets on which Behavioral Kinesiology rests are:
1. the primary importance of stress reduction and the associating emotional characteristics. All ailment is considered to be resulting from stress causing energy imbalances throughout the body system.
2. Stress if conditioned properly beginning from an early stage will prevent a lot of mental and attitudinal reactions, therefore, the essential role of Primary Prevention (prevention before the pathological cure, either mental or physical) cannot be overly emphasized in behavioral kinesiology.
3. The doctor is the teacher or guide to explain and give assistance to the patient, but it is the responsibility of the individual to take charge of his treatments and of his way of life.
4. High healing forces exists within us and in nature to enable repair to occur once the stress is reduced and the attitudes are corrected.
5. All problems start at the energy level.

Exploring The Sedona Method

This method focuses on emotions, attachments and its power or effects on us. It believes that our feelings control our lives and that we operate in the realms of those feelings. When one feels happy, there is this sense of strength, but when you are sad? You will move around down casted and sorrowful. Thus these feelings have begun to dictate our life, and our actions mirror them thereby preventing us from achieving our full potential.

The Sedona method has been used by many individuals to produce a flow of positive thinking while releasing years of amassed negativity. To live a happier, more relaxed life and a more productive life, Sedona Method techniques will be of great benefit to that end.

This procedure of releasing painful emotions was founded by Lester Levinson some 42 years ago. He was given a short while to live. Using the age-old spiritual methods to identify emotions and not thoughts as the reason behind suffering, he was able to heal himself!

The method of moving into a deeper peace can be summed as follows;
1) Let there be a recognition of the feeling
2) Let the feeling flow through you
3) Correctly identify that specific feeling
4) Settle into the feeling
5) Until finally the feeling releases.

How does it work?

Often we misinterpret our feelings and refuse to let them go. As we master the process of releasing, we realize that what we consider our deepest feelings are actually only on the surface. Deep down we have peace and quietness instead of these fears and pains. The first step is in acknowledging the source of the problem.

Sometimes our greatest pain is not with us in the present moment so avoid searching for it. Focusing on your sense of smell will fix your attention on the smells around you—thus you are living in the present! In the present, the mind is quite and at peace. Just listen. Listen deep to the surrounding silence deep within the sounds lies quietness. Focus in on the sounds around you. Pay attention to what you are seeing and allow yourself to appreciate and feel every vibrant color.

Now bring your focus to the very problem bothering you. Put in focus to every sound, thought, feelings and images associated with it. You will begin to realize or experience that the main problem is not what it was.

Releasing consciously

First, you will have to fix your mind on a particular problem that needs resolution. Give yourself a chance to feel whatever you are feeling is in this present moment. Ask yourself any one of the following three questions:

•Can I release this feeling?
•Can I allow this feeling to stay here?
•Can I welcome this feeling?

Yes or no are acceptable answers to these questions as they are merely asking you of the possibility of taking action. There is a need to ask yourself if you are willing to let go of the problem and be free or rather be chained to the feeling. Ask yourself a time frame based question. "When would I let go or release this feeling?" This should be repeated until the person is free of the feeling. If there is a resistance, repeat the preceding steps. While allowing yourself to feel the resistance or bad feelings fully. Don't cheat! Let go, only if you feel ready to let go. If you cheat or release before you're actually ready? It won't work.

- Can I free myself from the resistance to letting go?
- Would I let the feelings go?
- When would I let the feelings go?

Watch the feeling

Where does the feeling come from? The fear/want for
approval, love, admiration, care, safety, understanding, popularity, status quo etc.?

- Can you welcome the apprehension for that desire?
- Can you release the apprehension of that desire?
- Would you let go of the fear of losing or not having that desire?
- When?

Ask yourself the above questions. Identify if you're feeling arises from wanting to have control, be treated specially, feel secure, etc.

If you get an AUTHENTIC, congruent sign or answer from yourself, that it is ready to let go of it now? Then just release it! Release it as if you're, releasing dead skin, hair, dandruff, whiteheads, dirt from your skin etc. Those feelings may seem like they're a part of you? But they're not. They can simply be dropped and released if you recognize they're not attached to you.

Releasing Constantly

If you want to be truly free from painful or any undesired emotions is to make the releasing constant. For instance, you have a need to urinate every day to clear your system. You cannot hold the urine inside indefinitely as it causes damage to your kidneys. Likewise, instead of suppressing (keeping it in) or expressing (harming another person with it), choose rather to let the feelings go, as the feelings arise. Fix your mind on the feelings and ask yourself what they are, and let them all go.

The Splendid Benefits of Constant Releasing

You will have this feeling of happiness at all times and well rested than when you're suppressing your feelings. Your sense of pride fades, and the world seems more ideal. To gain freedom and lasting peace with the Sedona method as a beginner, just try it out for yourself and practice it often.   Make releasing constant and it will become a beautiful habit. Happiness, more success, a life without resistance, ease that comes from regularly releasing. To get significant effects, releasing once in a while unfortunately would not do. When constant releasing is done, The Sedona Method actualizes its promises or claims.

These six crucial steps must be held in l high regards;
1. More than your want for security, approval, separation, security and control -- grant yourself to want freedom more.
2. Take that decision to release and be free.
3. Realize that all your feelings cumulate in the selfish wants for security, control and approval and permit yourself to release each one.
4. Make the releasing constant, make sure to release these wants daily whether alone or with people.
5. If you encounter resistance, release the feelings or thoughts of being mentally stuck.
6. You will feel happier and lighter every time you release.

How to Release Your Feelings

1. **Head to heart movement**: Inhaling deeply, it will be better to begin from the center workhorse of emotions. Since the heart is considered the center, you work from your head (mental box) to your heart. Making a transition from what you think to what you feel. That is considered passing the opinion from the head to the heart.
2.   **Identify the feeling**
Choose the problem that bothers you, and ask yourself "what feeling is present right now?"
Try to resist any form of temptation to venture back into your mental box (head) and start thinking.
For instance, in considering the speech you are to deliver, ask yourself about your current feeling, "how so I feel about tomorrow's speech presentation right now?" Anxiety=worry. Then avoid using the head to awaken thoughts that are contrary to your ideal outcome. Sedona works in an amazing way that it affords you the chance of using feelings instead of getting tangled up with the complications of thoughts. But as the feelings dissolve, so do the thoughts.
3.   **Embrace the feeling**
Embrace a sense of acceptance. Ask yourself: "Could I welcome this feeling?" Allow the feeling (no matter how bad) to be fully present as possible, and with all gentleness

you can muster. Take note of what it feels like. For instance, you might feel anger as tension in your chest, or sadness as tightness in your throat. Or you may get more of what feels like an energetic sensation of constriction or not sense anything at all, which is fine. Often the feeling releases after this step.

Releasing by Letting Pent Up Emotions Go

Awareness of our real intentions by concentrating on our emotional. This is not intended to put someone into a perpetual state of apprehension or anticipation, but to only make us aware of our feelings, so that we can release them correctly. If these emotions are not released, negative emotions might simply become ignored, expressed or repressed in a negative way. Suppressed emotions often become expressed through other channels when the emotions become too much to contain and when the opportunity presents itself -- often when it's least expected. Releasing could be a means of opening these emotional "pressure valves" to release pent-up emotions.

Difference Between Releasing and Positive Thinking

Releasing offers a straightforward and efficient solution to this dilemma, by allowing you to release emotions and its underlying wants. While positive thinking involves a mental attitude whereby one expects good and favorable results. That is, positive thinking is the process of creating thoughts that will, in turn, create positive energy which will affect reality. A positive mind awaits happy endings in all situations. Positive thinking works in such a way that you tell a sick, dying man to think he is healthy and wait for his faith to make him healthy. Releasing concentrates on the very cause that is unravelling at the roots and freeing yourself from it.

Conclusion

Now that you have learned the techniques on this book I hope you can put this into action and as often as possible. Use it to remove as many issues as you have in your life. Use whatever techniques alongside EFT, Sedona, TFT and even CBT and compound them together for maximum effect. Personally I use these tools as complementary to positive change work. By that, I mean methodologies or systems used to create and INSTALL changes (as opposed to removing and erasing states) such as NLP and Hypnosis. These tools are indispensable and have their place. Positive change work plus releasing negatively pent up energy is an effectively powerful 1-2 punch. Some emotional problems are best solved on both sides simultaneously. One is to create positive change while dispersing or discharging the negativities from the opposite end of the spectrum. Whenever you can work on a problem from both sides, its more powerful because it has a layering effect, working on a problem on multiple layers. However, that is not to imply, on its own "eraser" type tools will not work on their own.

One Last Thing...

If you enjoyed this book or found it useful I'd be very grateful if you'd post a short review on Amazon. Your support really does make a difference and I read all the reviews personally so I can get your feedback and make this book even better.

If you'd like to leave a review then all you need to do is click the review link on this book's page on Amazon here:

Thanks again for your support!

This guide is not intended as and may not be construed as an alternative to or a substitute for professional business, mental counseling, therapy or medical services and advice

The authors, publishers, and distributors of this guide have made every effort to ensure the validity, accuracy, and timely nature of the information presented here However, no guarantee is made, neither direct nor implied, that the information in this guide or the techniques described herein are suitable for or applicable to any given individual person or group of persons, nor that any specific result will be achieved The authors, publishers, and distributors of this guide will be held harmless and without fault in all situations and causes arising from the use of this information by any person, with or without professional medical supervision The information contained in this book is for informational and entertainment purposes only It not intended as a professional advice or a recommendation to act

No part of this book may be reproduced or transmitted in any form whatsoever, electronic, or mechanical, including photocopying, recording, or by any informational storage or retrieval system without express permission from the author

Other books by JNR Publishing Group

84284583R00017

Made in the USA
Columbia, SC
15 December 2017